From Factory to Store

Anastasia Suen

rourkeeducationalmedia.com

*Scan for Related Titles
and Teacher Resources*

Teaching Focus:
One to One Correspondence- Point to each word as you read.

Before Reading:

Building Academic Vocabulary and Background Knowledge
Before reading a book, it is important to set the stage for your child or students by using pre-reading strategies. This will help them develop their vocabulary, increase their reading comprehension, and make connections across the curriculum.

1. *Read the title and look at the cover. Let's make predictions about what this book will be about.*
2. *Take a picture walk by talking about the pictures/photographs in the book. Implant the vocabulary as you take the picture walk. Be sure to talk about the text features such as headings, Table of Contents, glossary, bolded words, captions, charts/diagrams, or Index.*
3. *Have students read the first page of text with you then have students read the remaining text.*
4. *Strategy Talk – use to assist students while reading.*
   - *Get your mouth ready*
   - *Look at the picture*
   - *Think…does it make sense*
   - *Think…does it look right*
   - *Think…does it sound right*
   - *Chunk it – by looking for a part you know*
5. *Read it again.*
6. *After reading the book complete the activities below.*

Content Area Vocabulary
Use glossary words in a sentence.

assembly line
distribution center
factory
freight
order
trailers

After Reading:

Comprehension and Extension Activity
After reading the book, work on the following questions with your child or students in order to check their level of reading comprehension and content mastery.

1. *Why do the boxes of bicycles need a label? (Infer)*
2. *How do workers know how to build the bicycle? (Summarize)*
3. *Do you know how to ride a bike? Tell us about your bike. (Text to self connection)*
4. *Besides semi-trucks, what are other ways boxes of bicycles can make it from the factory? (Asking Questions)*

Extension Activity
Career Connection! There were many jobs mentioned in the book. Make a list of all the jobs found in the book. Which one seems interesting to you? Which would you choose and why? Ask your parents or classmates which job they would choose and why? Did you have the same choice as someone else? Is this what you want to be when you are a grownup?

How do all of these bikes get to the store?

Bicycles are made in a **factory**.

4

It all starts with an idea and plans.

Job Shop

Designers draw plans for a new bicycle.

The plans tell workers how to make each part.

Job Shop

Workers use machines to make the parts.

Some parts are welded together.

Job Shop

A welder uses heat to weld metal together.

One by one, each part of the bicycle is made. Each worker adds a new part.

When the bicycle's parts are all together, it is packed in a box.

Office workers take orders for the new bikes.

Job Shop

Stores order bicycles from the factory.

The forklift operator finds the bicycles for each **order**.

The bicycles are stored in the warehouse until they are sold.

A label is made for each box.

Ship to Postal Code

John's Bicycle Shop
123 Main Street
Vero Beach, FL
32963

13

A delivery truck picks up the orders.

The bicycles leave the factory.

Workers at the shipping company use machines to sort the boxes by their addresses.

Job Shop

*Every night, workers at shipping companies sort lots of packages. These packages are called **freight**.*

Some boxes go to the airport for a quick delivery.

Job Shop
Pilots fly the airplanes so the bicycles can be delivered tomorrow.

Some boxes go into semi-truck **trailers**.

The bike store owner is excited to get a new shipment of bicycles to sell in her shop.

Job Shop

The bike store owner signs for the delivery.

The mechanic puts the front wheel and seat on the bike.

Off we go!

 Photo Glossary

assembly line (uh-SEM-blee LAYHN): Workers in a line putting parts together to make something.

distribution center (dis-truh-BYOO-shuhn SEN-ter): A building where packages are sorted for delivery.

factory (FAK-tuh-ree): A building where things are made by people and machines.

freight (FREYT): Packages carried to another place by a plane, truck, or train.

order (AWR-der): To ask a factory to send you something.

trailers (TREY-lerz): A large van used to carry freight.

Index

assembly line 8

designers 5

distribution center 15

factory 4, 11, 15

forklift 12

mechanic 20

order 11, 12

store 3, 11, 19

trailers 18

Websites to Visit

www.cannondale.com

www.fedex.com/us/supply-chain/services/fulfillment-services/video.html

cyclefit.co.uk/usa-bike-factory-tour

Meet The Author!
www.meetREMauthors.com

About the Author

Anastasia Suen has been riding bicycles since she was a child and has visited many bicycle shops over the years. The author of 190 books for children, she lives with her family in Plano, Texas.

© 2015 Rourke Educational Media

www.rourkeeducationalmedia.com

PHOTO CREDITS: Cover: ©Corbis; cover (middle): ©Pressmaster; title page: ©XiXinXing; page 3: ©Izabela Habur; page 4, 22 (bottom): ©greatpapa; page 5: ©Vladyslav Starozhylov; page 6: ©Kobets Dmitry; page 7: ©Michael Luhrenberg; page 8-10, 22 (top): ©American Spirit; page 11, 19, 23 (middle): ©michaeljung; page 12: ©Eduard Andras; page 13: ©Steve Debenport; page 13: ©Jupiter Studio_1; page 14: ©Razuan Chisu; page 15, 23 (bottom): ©Gilles Lougassi; page 16: ©Monkey Business Images; page 17, page 23 (top): ©Pierre-Yves Babelon; page 18: ©Welcomia; page 20: ©Goodluz; page 21: ©gbh007; page 22: ©SteveDesign

Edited by: Luana Mitten
Cover design by: Jen Thomas
Interior design by: Rhea Magaro

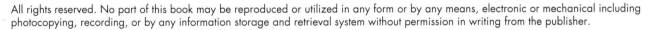

Library of Congress PCN Data

From Factory to Store/ Anastasia Suen
(Little World Communities and Commerce)
ISBN (hard cover)(alk. paper) 978-1-63430-060-5
ISBN (soft cover) 978-1-63430-090-2
ISBN (e-Book) 978-1-63430-117-6
Library of Congress Control Number: 2014953340
Printed in the United States of America, North Mankato, Minnesota

Also Available as: